W9-DIH-067

Copyright © 1980, 1981 by Children's Television Workshop. MUPPET Characters © 1980, 1981 Muppets, Inc. All rights reserved under International and Pan-American Copyright Conventions. ® Sesame Street and the Sesame Street Sign are trademarks and service marks of the Children's Television Workshop. Published in the United States by Random House, Inc., New York, and simultaneously in Canada by Random House of Canada Limited, Toronto, in conjunction with the Children's Television Workshop. Distributed by Funk & Wagnalls, Inc., New York, N.Y. Manufactured in the United States of America. 2 3 4 5 6 7 8 9 0 0-394-88762–X

Four volume edition 1986.

volume 4

BIG BIRD'S SESAME STREET® DICTIONARY

FEATURING JIM HENSON'S SESAME STREET MUPPETS

LETTERS R–Z

by Linda Hayward
illustrated by Joe Mathieu
Editor in Chief: Sharon Lerner

Art Directors: Grace Clarke and Cathy Goldsmith
with special thanks to Judith M. Leary

Funk & Wagnalls, Inc./Children's Television Workshop

Rr

A B C D E F G H I J K L M N O P Q **R** S T U V W X Y Z

rabbit A rabbit is a furry animal with long ears.

race A race is a contest to see who is the fastest.

The **rabbits** are about to have a **race.**

radio A radio is a machine. When you turn on a radio, you can hear music or voices.

Bert is listening to the Pigeon News on the **radio.**

railroad A railroad is a track for trains. A track is made with long metal strips called rails.

Look up the word train.

The **railroad** workers are working on the **railroad.**

Copyright © 1980, 1981 by Children's Television Workshop.
MUPPET Characters © 1980, 1981 Muppets, Inc.

rain Rain is water that falls in drops from clouds.

rainbow A rainbow is a strip of colors that you sometimes see in the sky when it rains.

raincoat A raincoat is a coat that keeps you from getting wet when it rains.

rake A rake is a tool used to make the ground smooth or clear.

Big Bird is using a **rake** to **rake** away the leaves.

ranch A ranch is a place for raising animals.

Rodeo Rosie lives on a **ranch.**

raw Food that is raw is not cooked.

Rodeo Rosie gives her horse **raw** carrots to eat.

reach When you reach, you stretch out a part of your body to take or touch something.

Cookie Monster can **reach** the cookie jar on the top shelf.

read When you read, you understand the words you see.

ready If you are ready to do something, you have everything you need to do it.

Hey, Bert! Are you **ready** to go to the costume party?
I'm **ready.**

Bert is not a **real** pigeon.
Bernice is a **real** pigeon.

real Real means true. A real thing is not make-believe.

really Really means truly.

That's a **really** scary monster costume you are wearing.
This is not a costume. I **really** am a monster.

reason When you know why something happens, you know the reason.

Give me a **reason** why I should believe you are a real witch.
Oh!

recipe A recipe tells you how to make something to eat.

record A record is a round, flat piece of plastic that can be played on a record player to make music.

rectangle A rectangle is a shape with four sides and four square corners.

Three of these shapes are **rectangles.**
A circle is not a **rectangle.**
The circle does not belong.

refrigerator A refrigerator is a machine that keeps food cold.

relative Your relatives are the people in your family.

remember When you remember, you think of something that happened in the past.

rent When you rent something, you pay to use it. You do not own it.

repair Repair means fix.

Prairie Dawn can **repair** a broken chair.

rest When you rest, you nap or stay quiet for a while.

Big Bird needs to **rest** every afternoon.

rest The rest of something is everything that is left.

Hey, waiter! There is only one letter in my alphabet soup. Where is the **rest** of the alphabet?
Here are the **rest** of the letters, sir!

restaurant A restaurant is a place where you can buy and eat a meal.

Grover the waiter works in a **restaurant.**

return When you return, you come back after being away. When you return something, you give it back.

I wonder when Ernie will **return.**
Sorry I'm late, Bert. I had to **return** the hammer I borrowed from Biff.

rhinoceros A rhinoceros is a big animal with thick skin and one or two horns on the top of its nose.

rhyme Words that rhyme sound alike at the end.

ribbon A ribbon is a narrow piece of cloth or paper.

Bert tied a **ribbon** around his present for Ernie.

rice Rice is a kind of grain. Rice grows above the ground in shallow water. Some cereals are made from rice.

Betty Lou is picking **rice.**

rich When you are rich, you have lots of money.

riddle A riddle is a question that is also a puzzle.

ride When you ride, you sit or stand while something carries you along.

Here's a monster **riddle.**
How can four big monsters **ride** in one tiny car?
Two in front and two in back!

right When something is right, it is correct. It is not wrong.

Grover, you had two big boxes, and I gave you two more. Now you have four big boxes. **Right?**
That's **right**!

right Right is also a direction. It is the opposite of left.

ring A ring is a circle.

Rodeo Rosie is in the center of the **ring.**

Ring around a Rosie ...
A **ring** that you wear is a circle that fits around your finger.

ring When something rings, it makes the sound of a bell.

Three of these things belong together.
One of these things is not the same.

A telephone, a cowbell, and a bicycle bell are things that **ring.** A banana does not **ring.** The banana does not belong.

river A river is a large stream of water that flows into another river, a lake, or an ocean.

Prairie Dawn is paddling her canoe up the **river.**

road A road is a man-made path between two places. It is wide enough for automobiles and trucks to ride on.

The Count is driving his bat car along the **road.**

robot A robot is a machine that can follow orders to do certain kinds of work.

Sam the **robot** can do many things that people can do.

rock A rock is a piece of stone. A rock is hard and comes out of the ground.

rock When you rock, you move back and forth or from side to side.

Farley likes to **rock** in a **rocking** chair.

rocket A rocket is a machine that moves through the air or up into space. Sometimes rockets go to the moon or other planets.

The **rocket** is taking off.

USA

rodeo A rodeo is a show in which cowgirls and cowboys ride horses and rope steers.

Come and see the **rodeo**!

roll When something rolls, it turns over and over as it moves along.

Betty Lou's ball started to **roll** down the hill, and Barkley chased it.

roof A roof is the top covering for a building.

Biff is fixing the **roof**.

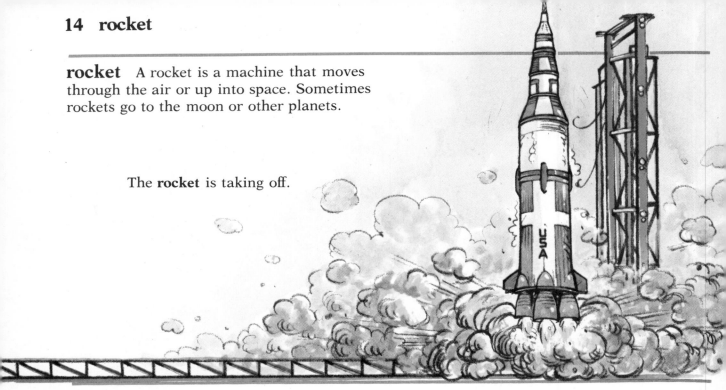

NAILS

room A room is space inside a building. A room is surrounded by walls.

This
room
belongs
to my cat,
Fatatatita.
FATATATITA

root A root is the part of a plant that is under the ground. Plants take in food through their roots. Some roots can be eaten.

Rose
Carrot

rope A rope is a strong, thick cord that can be used to tie things together.

Herry Monster forgot to untie the **rope.**

rough Rough means not smooth.

This ground
is very **rough**
and bumpy.

round Something round is shaped like a ball or a circle.

Three of these things belong together.
One of these things is not the same.

Pigeon Lover's Guide

An orange, a ring, and a wheel are **round.**
A book is not **round.**
The book does not belong.

row A row is a line of people or things.

There is a **row** of birds on Bert's clothesline.

row When you row, you move a boat by pulling oars through the water.

Herry likes to **row** his **row**boat.

rubber Rubber is something that stretches and is waterproof. Many things are made out of rubber.

rug A rug is a cover for the floor. A rug can cover the whole floor or a part of it.

Bert likes to vacuum the **rug.**

ruler A ruler is a tool with straight edges. It is used for measuring length. Look up the word length.

This board is two feet long.

The carpenter is using a **ruler.**
She is measuring the length of a board.

run When you run, you move very quickly on your feet.

Marshal Grover can **run** fast.
Fred can **run** faster.

Whoa, Fred! Wait for me!

This is ridiculous! How can you have a dictionary without words like rude and rubbish and rotten? I am going to read something *really* interesting.
THE ROTTEN EGG AND I

A B C D E F G H I J K L M N O P Q R **S** T U V W X Y Z

sad When you are sad, you feel unhappy.

Big Bird is **sad.**
He did not
get a letter from
Snuffle-upagus.

safe Safe means not in danger.

The little pig is **safe.**
The big bad wolf cannot
blow his house down.

sail A sail is a piece of cloth
that catches the wind.

sailboat A sailboat is a boat
with one or more sails.

Prairie Dawn's
sailboat has
one **sail.**

salt Salt is tiny white grains that come
from the ground or from sea water. Some
people put salt on food because they like
the way it tastes.

Sully is shaking **salt**
on his hard-boiled egg.

same When things are the same, they are like each other.

Cookie and Grover are wearing the **same** tie.

sand Sand is made of tiny grains of rock. You can find sand in the desert or at the beach.

Betty Lou likes to play in the **sand** at the beach.

sandwich A sandwich is two pieces of bread with some other food in between.

Here is my favorite **sandwich**— sardines and sour pickles on stinkweed bread!

save When you save something, you keep it in a safe place.

Bert **saves** bricks.

save Save also means to rescue someone or something from danger.

Uh-oh! There is someone who needs my help. I will **save** her.
HELP! HELP! Somebody **save** me from this furry blue monster!

saw A saw is a tool. It is made of metal and has teeth for cutting.

Prairie Dawn is cutting a board with a **saw.**

say Say means speak.

Ernie, why are you wearing earmuffs in the house?
What did you **say,** Bert? I can't hear you because I'm wearing earmuffs.

scale A scale is a machine that is used to weigh people or things.

Snuffle-upagus is standing on a **scale.** How much does he weigh?

scare Something that scares you is something that makes you afraid.

BOO!
Did I **scare** you? Heh, heh, heh.

school A school is a place where you go to learn things from teachers.

When I was a little count, I went to **school** to learn to count.
1 ... one wonderful **school**!

scissors Scissors are a tool used for cutting. Scissors have two handles and two blades.

I am cutting out paper birdies with my **scissors.**
Snip
Snip
Snip

scream When you scream, you make a loud noise with your voice.

EEEEE!
Don't **scream,** Betty Lou. There is nothing to be afraid of. It's only me, Herry.
I'm not afraid. I'm **screaming** because you are standing on my foot.

sea A sea is a very large body of salt water.

season A season is a time of the year.
There are four seasons: winter, spring, summer, and fall.

Farmer Grover works hard every **season.**

seat A seat is something to sit on.

Three of these things belong together. One of these things is not the same.

The stool, the chair, and the bench are all kinds of **seats.** A cactus is not a good thing to sit on. The cactus does not belong.

second A second is a very small amount of time. There are sixty seconds in a minute.

The Count is counting the **seconds** on his bat clock.

second Second also means the one that comes right after the first.

Betty Lou is first in line. Barkley is **second.**

secret A secret is a special thing you know but do not tell.

I have a special hiding place, but you do not know where it is. It is my **secret.**

see When you look at something, you see it.

seed A seed is the special part of a plant that can grow into a new plant.

Farmer Grover plants **seeds** in the spring.

selfish If you are selfish, you care about yourself and not about other people.

Cookie Monster! Don't be **selfish**! The cookies are for everyone.
COOKIES

sell When you sell something, you give it to someone and that person gives you money for it. After you sell something, it does not belong to you anymore.

I have to **sell** some of my old trash to make room for my new trash.
GARBAGE SALE

send When you send something, you start it on its way.

set A set is a group of things that are alike in some way.

I have a **set** of blue dishes.
I have a **set** of yellow dishes.

seven Seven is a number. Seven is one more than six.

seventeen Seventeen is a number. Seventeen is ten plus seven more.

Bert has ten red bricks and **seven** gray bricks. He has **seventeen** bricks all together.

sew When you sew, you use a needle to pull thread through cloth or other material. You can sew by hand or by machine.

The Amazing Mumford has to **sew** a new button on his cape.

shadow A shadow is a dark shape. When a light shines on something, it makes a shadow on the other side.

Egad! Look at that **shadow** on the wall. I think someone is following me.

shake When you shake something, you move it quickly back and forth or up and down.

Ernie has to **shake** the dust out of the mop.

shallow Something that is shallow is not deep.

The water in this wading pool is too **shallow** for swimming.
Not if you are a little bird.

shape The form of something is its shape.

share When you share something, you let others use it or have part of it.

Here, Sully. I will **share** my sandwich with you if you will **share** that apple with me.

sharp Something that is sharp has a thin cutting edge or a point on the end.

Hey, you! Wanna buy this knife? It's so **sharp,** it will cut, peel, slice, chop, saw....
I don't want to buy a knife. But how much is all that wonderful garbage??

she She is another way to say woman or girl or female animal.

Prairie Dawn is busy. **She** is making a home for her pet spider.

sheep A sheep is an animal that has four legs and is covered with wool.

I am a baby **sheep.** I am a lamb.
I am the lamb's mother. I am a ewe.
I am the lamb's father. I am a ram.

shell A shell is a hard covering. Some animals have shells. Some eggs have shells. Some seeds have shells.

Oscar, look at my collection of sea**shells.**
I have a **shell** collection, too, Betty Lou—egg**shells**!

shine When something shines, it makes a bright light. Something can also shine if light bounces off it.

Marshal Grover's badge **shines** because it is so clean.

ship A ship is a large boat. Some ships have sails and some have engines. Some have both.

Captain Bert's **ship** is sailing into the harbor.

shirt A shirt is a piece of clothing you wear on the top part of your body.

shoe A shoe is something you wear on your foot.

Ernie is wearing a striped **shirt** and one saddle **shoe.**

shop A shop is a store where you can buy things.

Cookie Monster loves to go **shopping** at the cookie **shop.**

short Something that is short is not as high as something that is tall.

When something is short, the beginning is close to the end.

Big Bird is tall.
Little Bird is **short.**
Little Bird's jump rope is too **short** for Big Bird.

shoulder Your shoulder is a part of your body. Your arms are attached to your shoulders. Look up the word body.

The Count's pet bat is sitting on his **shoulder.**

shout When you shout, you call out loudly.

MUD! FRESH MUD! GET YOUR MUD HERE!
I love to hear the Mudman **shout.**
FRESH MUD

shovel A shovel is a fool used to scoop things up.

Farmer Grover is using his snow **shovel** to **shovel** snow.

show When you show something, you put it where it can be seen.

Let me **show** you my seashell collection.
Let me **show** you my nutshell collection.

show A show is something special to be seen or heard. A show can be a movie, a play, or a program on radio or television.

Grover Knover is putting on a **show.** Everyone is watching.

shut When you shut something, you close it.

I must **shut** the barn door so the cows will not get out.

sick When you are sick, you are not healthy.

Biff is **sick.** He has a cold.

side The side of something is the part that is not the top, bottom, front, or back.

Herry Monster is lifting a chest. There are two handles—one on each **side.**

sign A sign tells you something. A printed sign uses words or pictures. You can also make signs with your hands in special ways.

What do these **signs** tell you?

STOP
When you **sign** your name, you write your name.

silent Silent means without any sound.

Shhhhh! We must be **silent** while Mr. Snuffle-upagus takes his nap!
ZZZ

silly When something is silly, it does not make sense and may be funny.

Fred, what happened to your head?

Isn't Marshal Grover **silly**?

sing When you sing, you make music with your voice.

Bert likes to **sing** to Bernice. Bernice thinks he is a good **singer.**

Doin' the Pigeon ...

single Single is a word that means one.

I would like a **single** scoop of birdseed ice cream, please.

sink A sink is a bowl that can be filled with water and has a drain to let the water out.

Cookie the baker has a **sink** full of dirty dishes.

sink When something sinks, it goes down. In water, some things float and some things sink.

Grover's rowboat is beginning to **sink.**

sister If your mother and father have another child who is a girl, she is your sister.

She is my **sister.**
He is my brother.

sit When you sit, you rest on the lower part of your body. Your weight is off your feet.

Why did the monster **sit** on the clock?
He wanted to be on time!
crunch!

six Six is a number. Six is one more than five.

sixteen Sixteen is a number. Sixteen is ten plus six more.

Oscar has ten red apple cores and **six** green apple cores. He has **sixteen** apple cores all together.

size The size of something is how big or how small it is.

Figgy Fizz comes in three different **sizes**—small, medium, and large.
Figgy Fizz

skate A skate is something you wear on your foot to help you move on ice, hard floors, or sidewalks. Some skates have runners and some have wheels.

Betty Lou wears roller **skates** to **skate** on the sidewalk.

Farley wears ice **skates** to **skate** on the ice.

skeleton Your skeleton is all the bones of your body fitted together. All people and most animals have skeletons. Look up the word bone.

skin Your skin is the outer covering of your body. Animals and fruits and vegetables also have skins.

My pet snake, Sammy, has pretty stripes on his **skin.**
I do not have stripes on my **skin.**

skip When you skip, you take little hops while you run.

I like
to walk.
I like
to **skip.**

When you **skip** something, you leave it out.
I read the whole dictionary and didn't **skip** one word.

skirt A skirt is a piece of clothing. It hangs from your waist.

Rodeo Rosie is wearing a brown **skirt.**

sled A sled is something with runners that slides on the snow or the ice.

Betty Lou is coasting down the hill on her **sled.**

sky The sky is the covering of air and clouds over the world.

I love to fly my little airplane in the **sky.**

sleep When you sleep, you close your eyes and rest your whole body.

Grover likes to **sleep** with his teddy bear.

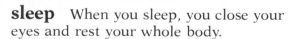

slide Slide means to move smoothly across a surface.

slide A slide is a playground toy. After you climb to the top, you slide to the bottom.

Big Bird likes to **slide** down the **slide.**

slip When you slip, you slide and start to fall.

slippery Something that is slippery can make you slip.

ooOOPS!
Banana peels are **slippery.** If you step on one, you may **slip.**

slow Slow means not fast.

Barkley is watching a snail race. Snails are **slow.**

small Small means little.

Big Bird has a large mailbox.

Little Bird has a **small** mailbox.

smell When you smell something, you breathe an odor in through your nose.

Can you **smell** my stinkweek soup? Doesn't it have a lovely **smell**?
PHEW!

smile When you smile, the corners of your mouth turn up and you look happy.

Rubber Duckie makes Ernie **smile.**

smoke Smoke is the cloud that rises from something burning.

Prairie Dawn's campfire is still burning. She can see the **smoke.**

smooth Something that is smooth has a surface that is not rough or wrinkled or bumpy.

The sidewalk is **smooth.**
The road is bumpy.

sneeze When you sneeze, air comes out of your nose and mouth and you make a loud sound like AH-CHOO.

Pepper makes you ... ah ... AH ... AH ... CHOOOO! ... **sneeze.**

snow Snow is tiny white flakes of frozen water that fall from the clouds.

so So means very.

I love
the **snow**—
so, so much.

soap Soap is something used with water to clean things.

Ernie is cleaning Rubber Duckie with **soap.**

sock A sock is something made of cloth that you wear on your foot. You put on your sock before you put on your shoe.

There is a hole in the Count's **sock.**

1 . . .
one hole!
Wonderful!

soft When something is soft, it is not hard or stiff.

Three of these things belong together. One of these things is not the same.

A teddy bear, a pillow, and a blanket are all **soft** things. A lunchbox is a hard thing. The lunchbox does not belong.

son If a father and mother have a child who is a boy, that child is their son.

song A song is something to sing.

soon Soon is a word that means not too long from now.

sorry When you are sorry, you are sad about something that has happened.

sound A sound is something you hear.

soup Soup is a liquid food made by cooking meat, vegetables, or fruits in water.

speak When you speak, you talk.

special Special is a word that means not like all the others.

speed The speed of something is how fast it goes.

Grover Knover can move with great **speed.**

spell When you spell a word, you say or write its letters in the right order.

Oscar can **spell** SCRAM.

spider A spider is a very small animal with eight legs. Many spiders spin webs to catch insects for food.

spill When something spills, it falls out of a container—usually by mistake.

Farley did not want to **spill** his jellybeans. But he did.

spin When you spin something, you turn it around and around quickly.
When something spins, it turns around quickly.

Ernie likes to **spin** his top.
His top is **spinning** fast.

spoon A spoon is a tool used to stir or scoop up food. You sometimes use a spoon when you eat.

Bert eats his oatmeal with a **spoon.**

spot A spot is a kind of mark.

spread When you spread something, you smooth it out so that it covers more space.

Bert likes to **spread** peanut butter on a piece of bread.

spring Spring is the name of a season. Spring comes after winter.

The leaves on the trees are beginning to grow. It must be **spring.**

square A square is a shape with four corners and four sides of the same length.

One of these shapes is not like the others. One of these shapes does not belong.

The circle does not have four corners and four sides. It is not a **square.** It does not belong.

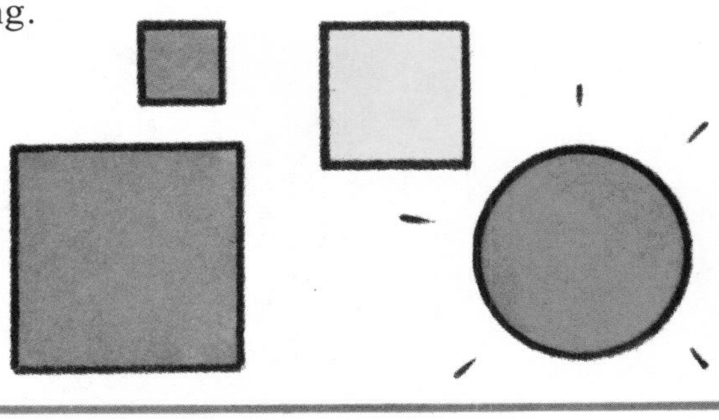

squeeze When you squeeze something, you press it.

Ernie has to **squeeze** the sponge to get the water out.

stage A stage is the place in the theater where the actors act, the dancers dance, and the singers sing.

Big Bird is acting on the **stage.**

stairs Stairs are a set of steps. You can go up stairs and you can go down stairs.

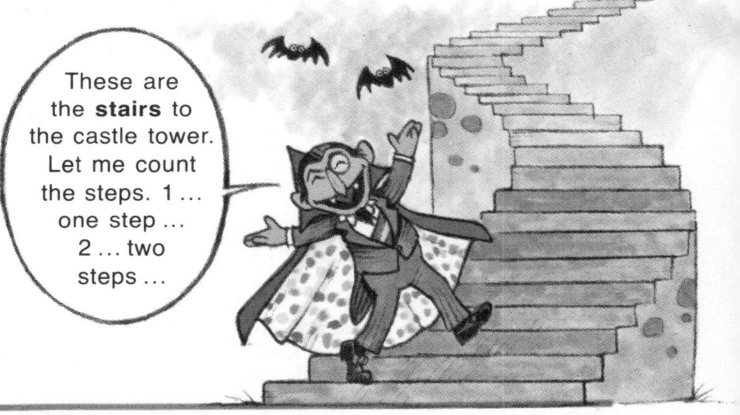

stamp A stamp is a small piece of paper that you put on a letter or package to show that you have paid to send it.

stand When you stand, you are on your feet, but your feet are not moving.

Farley has to **stand** in line to buy a **stamp** for his letter.

star A star is another sun—far, far away. At night a star looks like a tiny point of light in the sky.

Grover the astronaut can see many **stars.**

star A star is also a shape.

Grover's spaceship has a **star** on its side.

start When you start something, you begin it or get it going.

Grouches, **start** your grouchmobiles so I can **start** the race.
STARTER
START

stay When you stay, you do not leave.

Connie the witch is going on a trip. The other witches will **stay** at home.

steal When someone steals, that person takes something that does not belong to him or her.

step A step is what you put your foot on when you go up or down stairs.

The stairs in my castle have five hundred and sixty-eight **steps.** I love to count them all. 1 ... one **step** ... 2 ...two **steps** ...

string A string is a very thin rope.

Big Bird is tying a package with **string.**

strong Strong means having lots of power or not easily broken.

Herry can lift heavy barbells.
Herry is **strong.**

The third little pig's house was **strong.** The wolf could not blow it down.

subtract When you subtract, you take something away.

If I **subtract** one apple from four apples, I will have three apples.
4
-1
3

subway A subway is an underground railroad. Some cities have subways.

Biff rides to work on the **subway.**

suddenly Suddenly means all at once.

The Monster Marching Band had to stop **suddenly.**

sugar Sugar is something you can put in food to make it taste sweeter.

This lemonade tastes too sweet. There is too much **sugar** in it.
SUGAR

summer Summer is the name of a season. Summer comes after spring.

sun The sun is a star. It gives light and warmth and energy to all living things on the earth.

The **sun** is the brightest light in the sky.

The days are getting longer and hotter. It must be **summer.**

super Super means extra-big, extra-strong, extra-smart, or extra-good.

I, **Super** Grover, am proud that I can help people with my **super** powers.
SUPER AWARD FOR SUPER GROVER
G

sure When you are sure about something, you know that it is true. You are certain.

surprise A surprise is something you do not know about or expect.

TELEPHONE
I am **sure** I saw Grover Monster go into that phone booth.
TELEPHONE
Super Grover! What a **surprise** to see you!

swallow When you swallow food or water, it goes down your throat to your stomach.

sweep To sweep means to brush away. You can use a broom to sweep dirt.

This is the way
I **sweep** my nest,
sweep my nest,
sweep my nest....

sweet When something is sweet, it is nice to taste or smell or hear or see. When something tastes sweet, it usually has sugar in it.

swim When you swim, you use your arms and legs to move through the water.

Prairie Dawn likes to **swim.**
She is a good **swimmer.**

swing A swing is a hanging seat that moves back and forth.

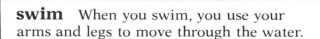

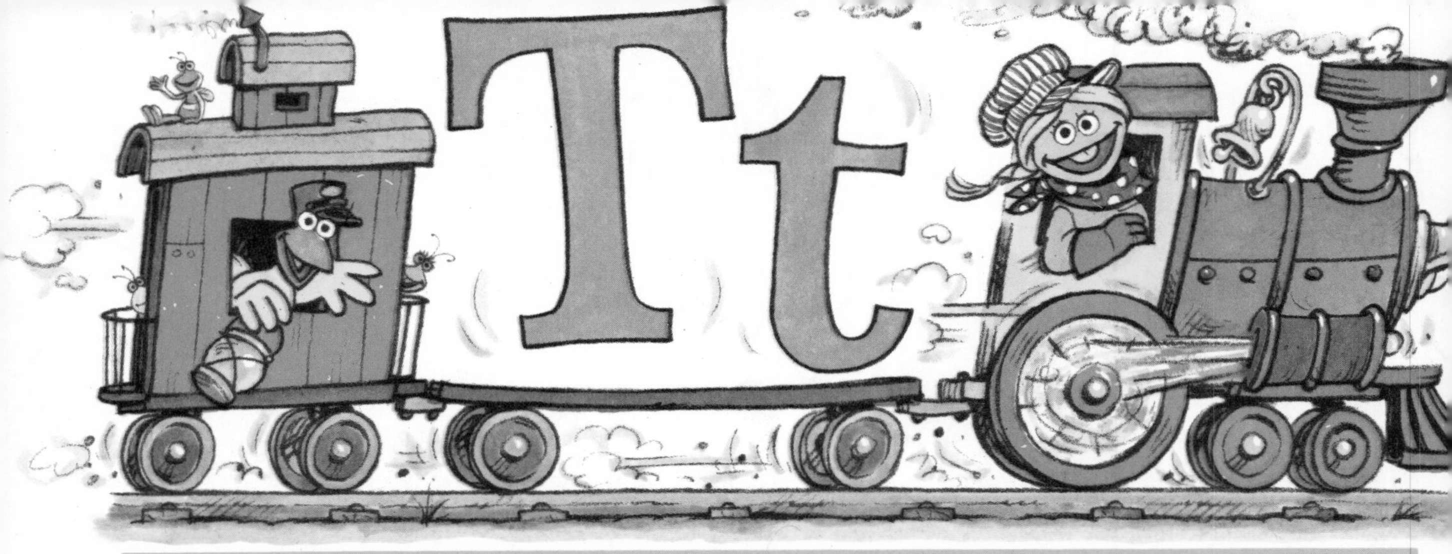

A B C D E F G H I J K L M N O P Q R S T U V W X Y Z

table A table is a piece of furniture with a flat top and legs.

Lay your cards on the **table,** Rosie!

tail A tail is a part of an animal's body. Some animals have tails and some animals do not.

Different animals have different kinds of **tails.**

I'm an animal, but I don't have a **tail.**

take When you take something, you catch hold of it, or have it with you when you go somewhere. Take also means do or make.

Oh, Mommy, I am so scared of the dark.
Don't be frightened, Grover, dear. **Take** my hand and I will **take** you home. Then you can **take** your bath.

talk When you talk, you say words.

Biff likes to **talk.** Sully likes to listen.

Hey, Sully, what do you have in your lunchbox? I have a peanut butter sandwich. I love peanut butter....

Copyright © 1980, 1981 by Children's Television Workshop. MUPPET Characters © 1980, 1981 Muppets, Inc.

tall Something tall is long from top to bottom. It is not short. The height of something is how tall it is.

taste When you taste something, you find out what flavor it has. You taste things with your tongue.

I can **taste** this lemon. It is sour.
I can **taste** this lollipop. It is sweet.

taxi A taxi is a special kind of car. You pay a taxi driver to drive you somewhere.

Bert and Ernie are going on a trip. They are taking a **taxi** to the airport.

teach When you teach, you help someone to learn.

teacher A teacher is someone who teaches—usually at a school.

Grover's **teacher** is trying to **teach** him how to write his name.

team A team is a group of people who work together to do the same thing.

My **team** is winning!
TUG of WAR CONTEST TODAY!

tear A tear is a tiny drop of water that comes from your eye when you cry.

Farley has **tears** in his eyes. He is crying because he dropped his apple in the sandbox.

tear When you tear something, you pull it apart.

I like to **tear** paper because **torn** paper is one of my favorite kinds of trash.
rrrrip!

telephone A telephone is used to send or receive sounds. When you use a telephone, you can talk to someone who is far away.

Big Bird is talking to Granny Bird on the **telephone.**

Gee, Granny. I sure like the birdseed cookies you sent to me.
I sure like the picture you sent to *me*, Big Bird.

television A television is a machine. When you turn on a television, you can see people and things and hear the sounds they make.

Bert is watching his favorite show on **television.**

tell When you tell something, you put it into words.

temperature The temperature of something is how hot or how cold it is. You use a thermometer to measure temperature.

Grover has a thermometer in his mouth. His mother is taking his **temperature.**

ten Ten is a number. Ten is one more than nine.

I have **ten** bats in my belfry.
10

thank When you thank someone, you say you like what that person did for you.

Gee, Barkley, I want to **thank** you for finding my other shoe.

that That means which or the one there.

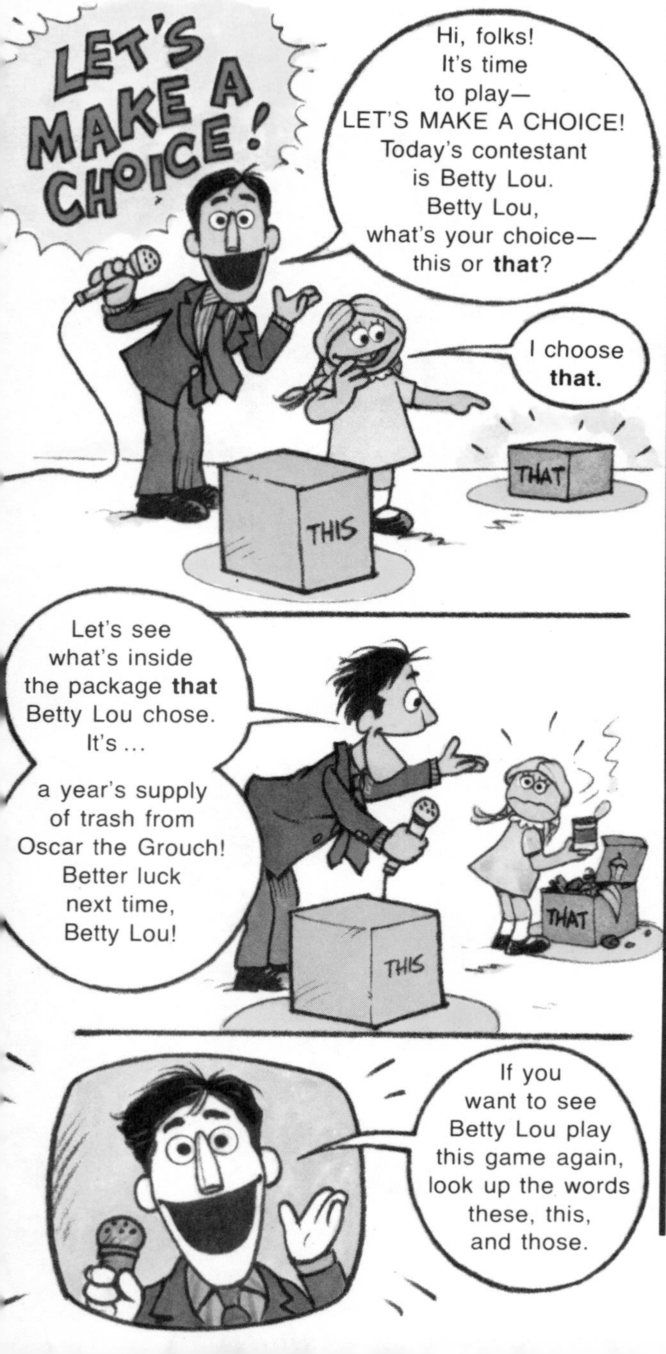

LET'S MAKE A CHOICE!
Hi, folks! It's time to play— LET'S MAKE A CHOICE! Today's contestant is Betty Lou. Betty Lou, what's your choice— this or **that**?
I choose **that.**
THIS
THAT
Let's see what's inside the package **that** Betty Lou chose. It's ...
a year's supply of trash from Oscar the Grouch! Better luck next time, Betty Lou!
THAT
THIS
If you want to see Betty Lou play this game again, look up the words these, this, and those.

the The means a certain one.

Bert, have you seen Rubber Duckie?
Do you mean **the** rubber duckie that I found in my paper clip collection, Ernie?
Bert's Paper Clip Collection

theater A theater is a place where you can see a play or a movie or another kind of show.

The Count is arriving at the **theater.**

their Their is another way of saying belonging to them. When something is theirs, it belongs to them.

them Them is another way of saying the ones I am talking about.

The Busbys are sitting on **their** bicycle.

then Then means at that time.

A long time ago there was a little girl named Miss Muffet who was sitting on a tuffet eating her curds and whey.
Then what happened?
Little Miss Muffet
Well, along came a spider who sat down beside her.
Then what happened?
Little Miss Muffet shared her curds and whey with the spider.

there There means in that place.

these These means the ones here.

they They means the people or things I am talking about.

LET'S MAKE A CHOICE!
Well, Betty Lou, are you ready to play LET'S MAKE A CHOICE? Here is today's choice. . . . What do you choose, Betty Lou—**these** or those?
I choose **these.**
THOSE
THESE
Then let's see what's inside **these** packages. Betty Lou, you chose . . .
a year's supply of sardine-and-sour-pickle sandwiches from Oscar the Grouch!
I don't like sardine-and-sour-pickle sandwiches. **They** make me sick.
THESE

thick When something solid is thick, it is big from side to side. When something liquid is thick, it is gooey and hard to pour.

thin When something is thin, it is not thick.

thing A thing can be seen or heard or touched or smelled. A thing can also be done or said or thought of.

Hand me that thick board, Sully. This board is too thin.
This paint is too thick.
This paint is too thin.
By the way, what is this thing we're building?
PAI

think When you think, you use your mind.

Hey, Bert. Does this beach umbrella make you think of building sand castles?
No, Ernie. It makes me think of vacuuming the rug. That beach umbrella was full of sand before you opened it.

thirsty When you are thirsty, you want something to drink.

Marshal Grover and Fred are **thirsty.**

Here you are— two big glasses of milk!

thirteen Thirteen is a number. Thirteen is ten plus three more.

Bert has three big boxes of oatmeal and ten small boxes of oatmeal. He has **thirteen** boxes of oatmeal all together.

LET'S MAKE A CHOICE!

this This means the one here.

those Those means the ones there.

Here's our contestant, Betty Lou, back to play— LET'S MAKE A CHOICE! Once more, Betty Lou . . . what do you choose— **this** or that or these or **those**?
This or that? These or **those**? **Those** or these? **This** or that? AARRRGGGHH! I can't stand it. Nothing! I choose nothing!
THAT
THOSE
THIS
THESE

Then let's see what you did not choose. In **this** package we find— a little puppy! In that package we find—a large bag of jellybeans! In these packages we find— cute, adorable kittens! And in **those** packages—a year's supply of coconut cream pies! I'm sorry, Betty Lou. And thanks for being such a wonderful contestant.
THAT
THIS
THESE

If you want to see what Betty Lou is thinking, look up the word thought.

thought A thought is an idea. A thought is what someone thinks.

Betty Lou's **thought:**

thread A thread is a thin piece of string used for sewing.

three Three is a number. Three is one more than two.

Farley is sewing **three** buttons on his shirt with **thread.**

through Through means from one side to the other side or from one end to the other end of something.

Barkley can jump **through** a hoop.

throw When you throw something, you toss it through the air.

When I **throw** the stick, Barkley runs after it.

thumb Your thumb is one of the fingers on your hand. Look up the word hand.

Ernie, why do you have a string tied around your **thumb**?
So I won't forget to buy more string.

thunder Thunder is the loud noise you sometimes hear when there is lightning. Look up the word lightning.

KA-BOOM!
Ahh. One lovely bolt of lightning and one fabulous clap of **thunder**! Wonderful!

ticket A ticket is a piece of paper that allows you to do something. Sometimes you pay money for a ticket.

tickle When something tickles you, it touches you lightly and makes you laugh.

Big Bird is riding on the train. The conductor is taking his **ticket.**

tie When you tie a string, rope, or ribbon, you put a knot or bow in it.

Ernie can **tie** his shoelaces.

A **tie** is something you can wear around your neck.

tiger A tiger is a big, wild orange cat with black stripes.

tight When something is tight, it fits too closely. It is not loose.

time Time is when something happens. Time is measured in seconds, minutes, hours, days, weeks, months, and years.

tired When you are tired, you need to rest.

to To means in the direction of.

Betty Lou is throwing a ball **to** Barkley.

today Today is the day it is now.

toe Your toe is a part of your foot. You have five toes on each foot. Look up the word body.

Bert is doing his exercises. He is touching his **toes.**

together Together means with each other.

tomato A tomato is a round red fruit that grows on vines above the ground.

Tomato
Hi, Oscar! We are all here **together** because it's your birthday today.
Have a Rotten Birthday
Here is a cake made out of mud.
And here's a present from all of us.
Wow! It's a rotten **tomato.** It's just what I wanted. Gee, thanks, everyone, for such a perfect birthday.

tomorrow Tomorrow is the day that comes after today.

I can't wait until **tomorrow.** Granny Bird just said she is coming to visit.
click

tonight Tonight is the night of the day that it is now.

tongue Your tongue is a part of your mouth. It helps you speak and taste.

Barkley likes to taste ice cream with his **tongue.**

too Too means also.

What is blue and furry and lovable and has eight wheels?
Grover on roller skates!
And I am *cute,* **too.**

too Too can also mean more than enough.

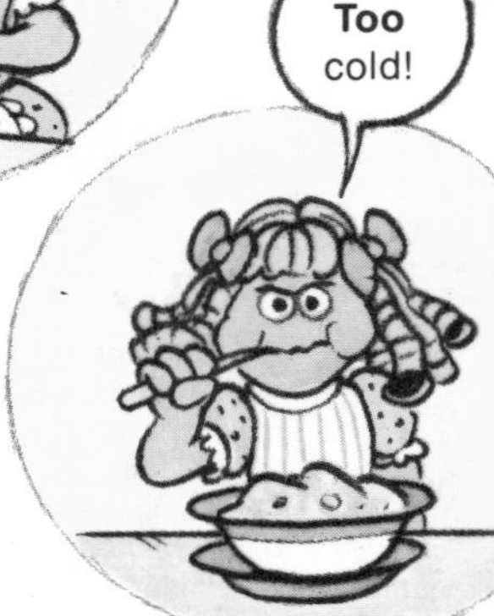

tool A tool is used to do work. Here are some different kinds of tools.

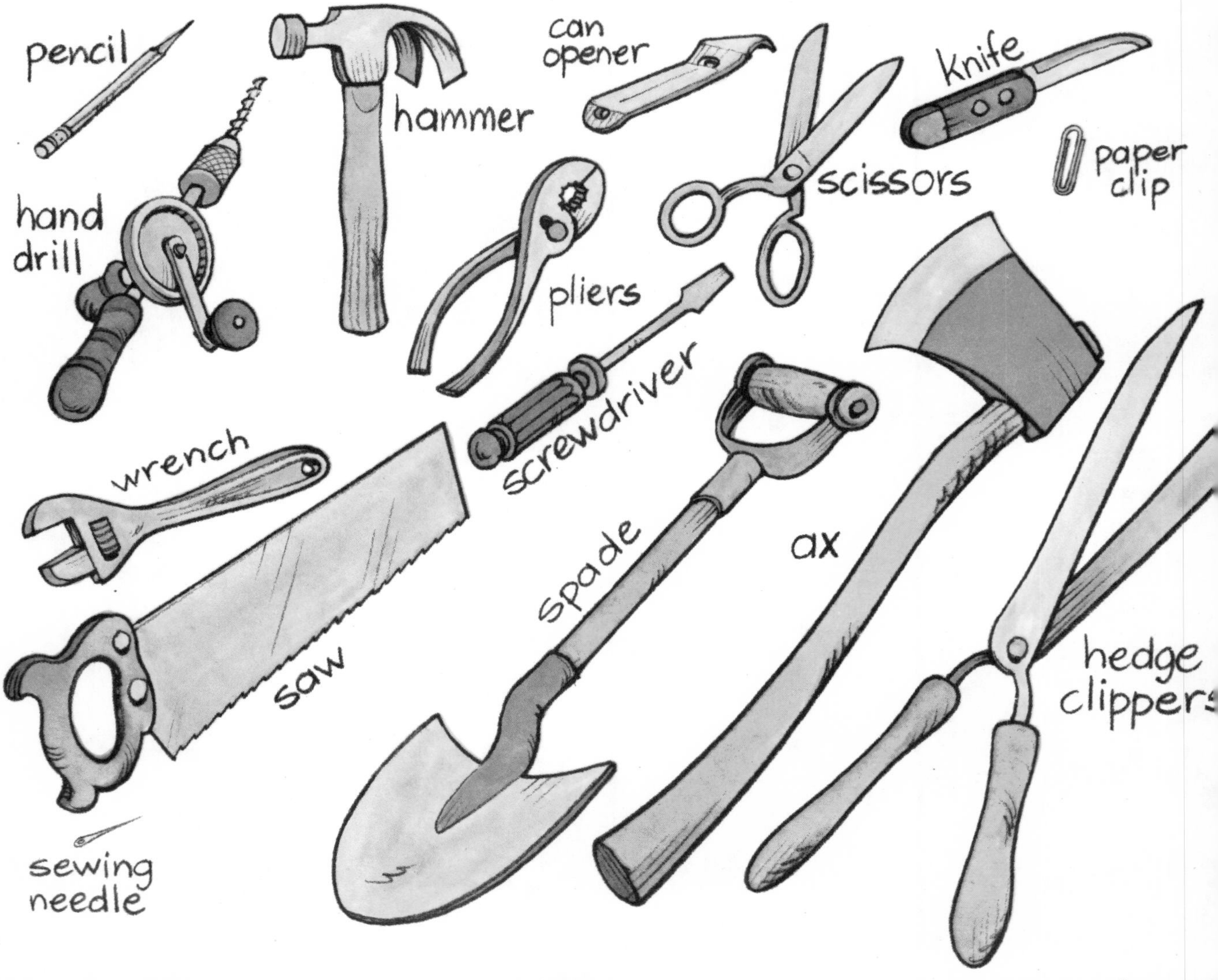

tooth A tooth is one of your teeth. Teeth are in your mouth and are used for biting and chewing.

Frazzle is brushing his **teeth.** He has one **tooth**brush for each **tooth.**

top The top of something is its highest part.

Where did you put my ball, Bert?
It's on the **top** of the toy chest, Ernie.
A **top** is also a lid. My jar has a blue **top**.

touch When you touch something, you feel it with your hand or another part of your body.

I love to **touch** my little lamb. He feels so soft.

towel A towel is a piece of cloth or paper that is used for drying something wet.

Herry Monster took a shower. He is drying himself with a **towel.**

town A town is a place where many people live and work. A town is usually smaller than a city.

Marshal Grover is riding into **town.**

toy A toy is something to play with.

Three of these things belong together. One of these things is not the same.

Rubber Duckie, a toy airplane, and a jack-in-the box are all **toys.** Bert's shoe is something to wear. Bert's shoe does not belong.

train A train is a string of railroad cars pulled along a track by an engine.

The cars have to stop so the **train** can go by.

trash Trash is things that are thrown away.

travel When you travel,
you go from one place to another.

Whenever I **travel,** I collect **trash** on the way.
ROAD CLOSED

tree A tree is a tall plant with a woody stem called a trunk.
A tree has branches and leaves or needles.

Who is hiding behind each **tree**?

triangle A triangle is a shape with three sides and three corners.

Three of these things belong together.
One of these things is not the same.
The square has four sides and four corners.
The square does not belong.

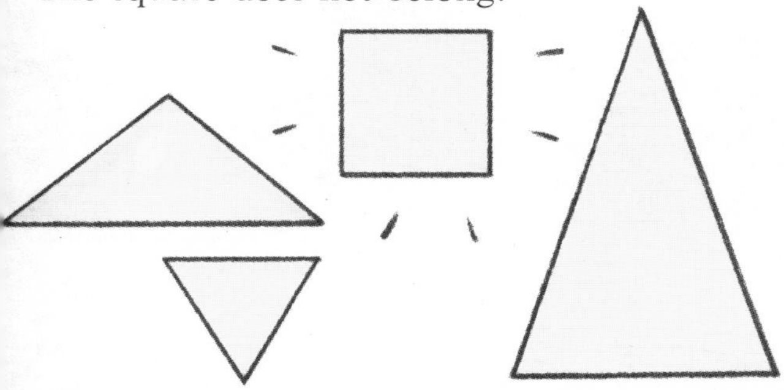

trip When you go on a trip, you travel somewhere.

Farley is going on a **trip.**
He is taking the train.

Have a nice **trip,** Farley.

trick A trick is a clever thing you can do.

The Amazing Mumford
is doing a magic **trick.**

trip When you trip, your foot bumps into something and you stumble or fall.

Grover, dear, be careful not to **trip** on the roller skate.
Oooops! You **tripped.**

tricycle A tricycle is something to ride. It has three wheels, a seat, handlebars, and pedals.

Barkley can ride a **tricycle.**

That is a good trick for a dog!

trouble When you are having trouble, you are having a problem.

Hey, Bert! I'm having **trouble** moving this box. What's in it?
Ernie, that's where I keep my rock collection.

truck A truck is a machine with an engine and four or more wheels. It is used to carry loads or do other kinds of work.

I just love to count **trucks.**

true When something is true, it is real. It is not false or a lie.

Is it **true** that a whale is the largest animal?
It's **true.**

trunk A trunk is a big suitcase.

trunk A trunk is also an elephant's nose.

trunk A trunk can also be the woody stem of a tree.

I, the Amazing Mumford, will now pull from this perfectly empty **trunk** two other **trunks.**
A LA PEANUT BUTTER SANDWICHES!
1, 2, 3. three trun Amazin

try When you try to do something, you make an effort to do it.

turn When something turns, it goes around and around or changes direction.

When I ride my bicycle, the wheels **turn** very fast.
When I **turn** a corner, I change direction.

turn When one thing turns into another thing, it becomes something else.

turtle A turtle is an animal with a hard shell and a soft body. A turtle can pull its head and arms and legs inside its shell.

Some people say that **turtles** can hide inside their shells and look just like rocks. Do you believe that?
Oh!

twelve Twelve is a number. Twelve is ten plus two more.

Bert has ten blue shoelaces and two orange shoelaces. Bert has **twelve** shoelaces all together.

twenty Twenty is a number. Twenty is ten plus ten more.

Ernie has ten red jellybeans and ten green jellybeans. Ernie has **twenty** jellybeans all together.

twin A twin is one of two children who have the same mother and father and are born at the same time. Some twins look exactly alike. Some twins do not look like each other.

The Busby **twins** look alike. The Henderson **twins** do not look alike.

two Two is a number. Two is one more than one.

There are **two** Busby twins.

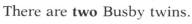

This dictionary is not as terrible as I thought. The T section has rotten tomatoes, garbage trucks, and trash, trash, trash!

Uu

A B C D E F G H I J K L M N O P Q R S T **U** V W X Y Z

ugly When you think something is ugly, you do not like to look at it or hear it.

umbrella An umbrella is a folding cover that protects you from the rain or the sun.

When can three big monsters fit under a tiny **umbrella** and not get wet?
When it is not raining.
RRRR!

uncle Your uncle is the brother of your mother or your father. Your aunt's husband is also your uncle.

under Under means below.

Super Grover is flying **under** the bridge. Little Bird is flying over the bridge.

understand When you understand something, you know what it means.

underwear The clothes you wear under your other clothes are called underwear. Undershirts and underpants are two kinds of underwear.

There are stars on the Amazing Mumford's **underwear.**

undress When you undress, you take off your clothes.

Ernie must **undress** before he can take a bath.

unhappy When you are unhappy, you do not feel happy—you feel sad.

Bert is **unhappy.** He lost his whole bottle cap collection.

until Until means up to the time of.

Farmer Grover always waits at the gate **until** the cows come home.

unusual Unusual means not usual. Something that is unusual is something that you are not used to seeing or hearing or feeling.

up When you go up, you move to a higher place.

I am going **up** the ladder.
I am going down the ladder.

upside down When something is upside down, the top is on the bottom and the bottom is on the top.

Big Bird is **upside down.**

us Us is another way of saying you and me.

use When you use a thing, you do something with it.

Hey, Bert. What does the word **use** mean?
Let's **use** the dictionary to find out.

usual Something that is usual is something that you are used to seeing, hearing, or feeling.

Bert is having his **usual** breakfast.

Bert, are you having oatmeal for breakfast *again?*

usually Usually means most often or in the ordinary way.

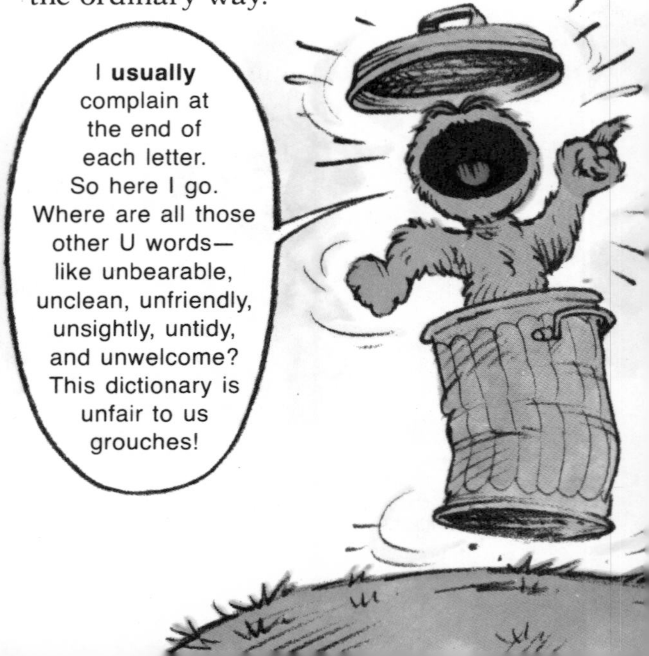

I **usually** complain at the end of each letter. So here I go. Where are all those other U words—like unbearable, unclean, unfriendly, unsightly, untidy, and unwelcome? This dictionary is unfair to us grouches!

Vv

A B C D E F G H I J K L M N O P Q R S T U V W X Y Z

vacation A vacation is a special time when someone does not work or go to school.

Guy Smiley is on **vacation.**

vacuum When you vacuum, you use a vacuum cleaner to suck up dust and dirt.

Bert likes to **vacuum** the rug.

valentine A valentine is a card that you send on Valentine's Day to someone you like.

Big Bird sent Snuffle-upagus a **valentine** on the fourteenth of February.

vase A vase is a container used for holding flowers.

Mr. Snuffle-upagus sent me a flower for Valentine's Day.

Big Bird put his flower in a **vase.**

vegetable A vegetable is a plant that is used for food.

Farmer Grover is picking **vegetables** in his **vegetable** garden.

very   Very means more than usual or much.

My dog is big, but Barkley is **very** big.

village   A village is a small town.

When the Count was born, his parents announced the news to all the people who lived in the **village.**

violin   A violin is a musical instrument. It has four strings and is played with a bow. Look up the word bow.

The Count loves to play the **violin.**

visit   When you visit, you go to see someone or something.

Prairie Dawn likes to **visit** the museum.

DON'T TOUCH!

voice   Your voice is the sound you make while talking or shouting or singing.

Hello, Bird!

I can hear Mr. Snuffle-upagus' **voice.**

Vacation is a word that begins with V. I would be very glad to take a vacation from this dictionary.

A B C D E F G H I J K L M N O P Q R S T U V W X Y Z

wagon A wagon is used to carry things. A wagon has four wheels and is usually pulled.

wait When you wait, you stop what you are doing or stay where you are until something happens.

Fred has to **wait** for Farmer Grover to load the **wagon.**

waiter A waiter is a person who takes orders and serves food in a restaurant.

Waiter! What is this fly doing in my soup?
He is doing the backstroke, sir.

Grover the **waiter** is serving alphabet soup.

wake When you wake, you stop sleeping.

ZZZZ
Wake up, Ernie! The Late Pigeon News is over. It's time to go to bed.

walk When you walk, you move by taking steps.

Grover Knover's motorcycle is broken. He has to **walk.**

wall A wall is the side of a building or a room. A wall can also be a kind of fence.

Biff and Sully are painting the **walls** of the room blue.

Oscar is building a **wall** around his trash can.

I **want** a **wall** around my trash can so people won't bother me.

want When you want something, you would like to have it.

warm When something is warm, it is more hot than cold. But it is not *very* hot.

The water in the bathtub is **warm**— just right for Rubber Duckie and me.

was Ernie **was** dirty. Now he is clean.

wash When you wash something, you clean it with water and sometimes soap.

Betty Lou likes to **wash** Barkley. Barkley does not like to be **washed.**

waste When you waste something, you do not make good use of it.

watch A watch is a small clock that you can wear on your wrist or carry in your pocket. A watch shows you what time it is.

Bert has a **watch** on his wrist.

watch When you watch something, you look at it.

Bert likes to **watch** the sun rise.

Today the sun is rising at six o'clock.

water Water is wet. We use water to drink, to cook with, and to clean with. All living things need water.

Herry Monster is taking a bath in hot **water.** He is drinking a glass of cold **water.**

way The way you do something is how you do it.

This is the **way** Ernie makes his bed.

This is the **way** Bert makes his bed.

way The way you go is the direction or path in which you move.

we We is another way of saying you and I.

weak Something that is weak breaks easily or is not strong.

The toy wagon is **weak.** It will not hold Barkley.

wear When you wear something, you have it on your body.

Marshal Grover **wears** a hat, a vest, chaps, and a shiny badge.

weather Weather can be sunny, cloudy, rainy, windy, or snowy. The weather is also how hot or how cold it is outside.

The mail carrier has to deliver the mail in all kinds of **weather.**

U.S. MAIL
Through rain or snow or sleet or hail, I see that Sesame Gulch gets the mail.

week A week is seven days long. Each day in the week has a special name. Look up the word calendar.

Bert has a busy **week.**

SUNDAY—Take Bernice for a walk.
MONDAY—Work on my bottle cap collection.
TUESDAY—Work on my paper clip collection.
WEDNESDAY—Buy oatmeal.
THURSDAY—Clean closet.
FRIDAY—Go To Pigeon Lovers' meeting.
SATURDAY—Polish saddle Shoes.

weigh When you weigh something, you find out how heavy it is.

weight The weight of something is how heavy it is. Your weight is how heavy you are.

Stand still, Farley. I want to **weigh** you. This scale will tell me your **weight.**

well When you are well, you are not sick. You are healthy.

Farley is **well.**

You are very healthy, Farley.
When you do something **well,** you do it in a good way.
I roller skate **well.**

were The Busby twins **were** at the zoo.

ZOO
ZOO
ZOO
We **were** both at the zoo yesterday.
You **were** there, too.

wet When something is wet, it has water or another liquid on it. It is not dry.

Barkley is **wet.**

Now everyone is **wet.**

whale A whale is a huge animal that lives in the ocean and looks like a fish. But it is not a fish. A whale breathes air.

AQUARIUM
The dictionary says that a **whale** looks like a fish but is not a fish.

what What is a word used to ask questions or talk about people and things.

What are you holding behind your back?
I have **what** my mother gave me for lunch.

wheel A wheel is something that is shaped like a circle and can roll or turn.

Three of these things belong together.
One of these things is not the same.

The wagon, the tricycle, and the roller skates are all things that have **wheels.**
The sled does not have **wheels.**
The sled does not belong.

when When is a word used to ask questions or talk about time.

When does Cookie Monster *not* want a cookie?
When he wants *two* cookies!

where Where is a word used to ask questions or talk about places.

Where do you go to buy clothes?
I go where all the monsters go— to the Monster Department Store.
THE MONSTER DEPT. STORE

which Which is a word used to ask questions or talk about people or things.

Which pair of shoes do you want?
I know which pair— the pair that fits me.

while While means during the time of.

whisper When you whisper, you say something very quietly.

Ernie has to **whisper** **while** the Pigeon News is on.

whistle A whistle is something that makes a loud, shrill sound when air is blown through it.

Herry Monster likes to blow his whistle.

whistle When you whistle, you make a loud, shrill sound by blowing air through your lips in a special way.

Sully likes to **whistle** while he works.

who Who is a word used to ask questions or talk about people.

Who lost this feather? The bird who lost this feather must be very big.

whole The whole of something is all the parts of it together.

I have a whole orange.
I have half an orange.

whose Whose is a word used to ask questions or talk about things that belong to people.

Egad! Footprints! **Whose** footprints are these?
I know **whose** footprints these are. Mine.

why Why is a word used to ask or talk about the reason for something.

wide How wide something is means how far it is from one side to the other. When something is wide, it is not narrow.

This doorway is not **wide** enough for me. It is too narrow.

wife A wife is a woman who is married.

She is my **wife.**
He is my husband.

will If you will do something, you are going to do it.

If you **will** say BLECCH very loudly, I **will** let you taste my ooky-gooky stew.
BLECCH!

win When you win a game or a race, you finish ahead of the others.

wind Wind is air that is moving.

window A window is an opening in a building or a vehicle to let in air or light. Most windows have glass in them.

Bert is looking out the **window**.

wing A wing is the part of birds, bats, and some insects that helps them fly. Airplanes also have wings.

winter Winter is the name of a season. Winter comes after fall.

wish A wish is something that you hope will come true. When you wish for something, you want it.

witch A witch is a person with magical powers. Many fairy tales have witches in them.

Connie the **witch** is reading a story.

with With means using or having. With also means in the company of.

woman A woman is a grown-up girl.

There is one **woman,** one girl, and one monster in the elevator.

wonder When you wonder about something, you would like to know about it.

wonderful Something wonderful is surprising or amazing. Sometimes the word wonderful is used to mean very good.

That's wonderful!

wood Wood is the hard part of a tree. Many things are made of wood.

I like to build things with wood.

word A word is a group of letters or sounds that has a meaning. You can say a word or read it.

There are so many words that begin with W. WOW!
THE SESAME STREET DICTIONARY

work When you work, you do something that uses energy. Most people work at jobs to earn money.

I work at the post office.
U.S. MAIL

Special
I work at the grocery store.

I work at the hospital.

I work at the factory.

I work at school.
MATH

I am not working. I am resting.

world A world is a planet. Our world is the planet earth.

I can see the whole world from my little spaceship.

worm A worm is a tiny animal with a long, soft body and no legs. Earthworms live under the ground.

Slimey is my pet **worm.**

worry When you worry, you are afraid that something bad is going to happen.

Be careful, Ernie! Those cups are going to fall.
You **worry** too much, Bert.

wrap When you wrap something, you cover it.

I have to **wrap** this present for Mr. Snuffle-upagus.

write When you write, you put words on something—usually paper.

writer A writer is someone who writes stories, letters, or other things for people to read.

Herry is a **writer.** Does he **write** with his left hand or his right hand?
I **write** with a pencil.

wrong When something is wrong, it is not correct. It is not true.

Farley has four apples. Right or **wrong**?
Wrong! I have only three apples.

I wonder where the words wart, weed, whimper, and whine went.

A B C D E F G H I J K L M N O P Q R S T U V W X Y Z

x-ray An x-ray is a picture of the inside of something. Sometimes the doctor takes an x-ray of your body to see if anything is wrong inside.

The doctor took an **x-ray** of Mr. Hooper's chest.

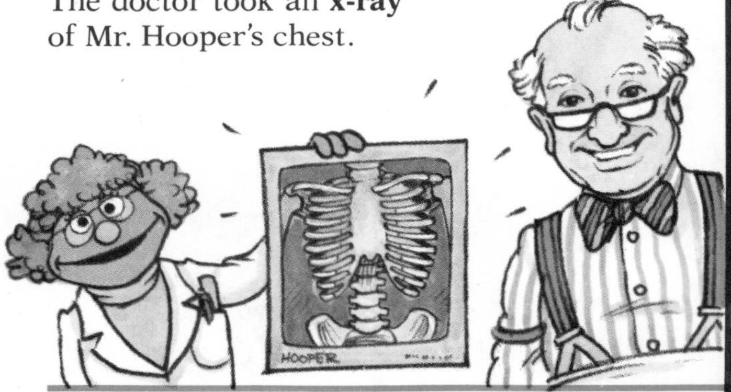

xylophone A xylophone is a musical instrument with two rows of wooden bars that you hit with wooden hammers.

Frazzle likes to play the **xylophone.**

yard A yard is a piece of ground next to a house or a school or another kind of building.

Biff and Sully are building a fence around their **yard.**

yawn When you yawn, you open your mouth wide and take a deep breath. You yawn because you are tired or bored.

YAWN!
And I found this bottle cap on the sidewalk one day when I was walking home from the store. I had just bought some oatmeal . . . .

Bert's stories make Ernie **yawn.**

year A year is an amount of time that is three hundred and sixty-five days long. A new year begins with January and ends with December. Look up the word calendar.

Today is my birthday. Now I will have to wait a whole **year** for my next birthday.

yell When you yell, you cry out loudly.

Cookie Monster **yells** KOWABUNGA when he sees a pile of cookies.

yes Yes is a word you use to say that something is true. You can also use yes to say you will or can do something.

Cookie Monster, do you want a cookie?
YES!

yesterday Yesterday is the day that came before today.

you You means the person or persons spoken to.

This belongs to **you,** Ernie.
These belong to **you,** Bert.

young Someone who is young has lived a short time. A young person has not lived as long as someone who is old.

Farley is **young,** but his baby brother is **younger.** Their grandfather is old.

your Your is another way of saying belonging to you.

yours When something belongs to you, it is yours.

Is this **your** umbrella, Little Bird?
Yes, that's mine. Is this **yours**?

yourself Yourself is sometimes used instead of you.

Mommy, I fell down.
Did you hurt **yourself,** Grover, dear?

Yo-Yo™ A Yo-Yo is a toy that goes up and down on a string.

Betty Lou is trying to win the **Yo-Yo** contest.

zebra A zebra is a white animal with black stripes. A zebra has four legs, a mane, and a tail.

zipper A zipper is something that is used to fasten clothes or other things.

Ernie, please help me **zip** the **zipper** on my jacket.
Sure, Bert. But first I have to un**zip** the **zipper** on my sleeping bag.
ZIP!

zoo A zoo is a place where animals are kept so that people can see them.

Big Bird likes to visit the animals at the **zoo.**

To the
PIGEON
HOUSE

HURRAY!
There are no more words left in this yucchy dictionary!

But now I don't have anything else to complain about.
I think I'll go back to A and start over again.

Gee, Big Bird, I never knew a dictionary could be so much fun! I'm going to look at all four books again—starting right now!

Oh, I'm so happy you liked my dictionary, Little Bird! And I like to look at it again and again. Every time I do, I see something new . . . and I bet you will too!

Aa Bb Cc
Dd Ee
Ff Gg Hh
Ii Jj Kk
Ll Mm